DOUBLE BASS

T0165097

AN ESSENTIAL ELEMENTS METHOD

ADVANCED TECHNIQUE
FOR STRINGS

Technique and style studies for string orchestra

FLEXIBLE SEQUENCE FORMAT
Choose pages from the 4 major sections:

I. **Scales and Arpeggios**
II. **Shifting Studies**
III. **Rhythm and Bowing Studies**
IV. **Musical Styles**

BY

MICHAEL ALLEN • ROBERT GILLESPIE • PAMELA TELLEJOHN HAYES

Double Bass consultant and editor
DR. PAUL ROBINSON

ISBN 978-0-634-01055-2

HAL•LEONARD® CORPORATION
7777 W. BLUEMOUND RD. P.O. BOX 13819 MILWAUKEE, WI 53213

READING TENOR AND TREBLE CLEF

DOUBLE BASSES ONLY

TENOR CLEF

Double basses sometimes read notation in tenor clef, which is indicated by the sign 𝄡 and centered on the 4th staff line.

The following pitches are played in the same places on your instrument.

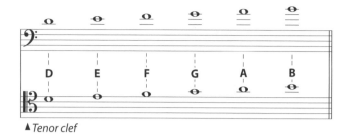

▲ *Tenor clef*

The tenor clef is often used to avoid too many ledger lines.
The following examples demonstrate how the tenor clef eliminates ledger lines.

TREBLE CLEF

Double basses sometimes read notation in treble clef, which is indicated by the sign 𝄞 and centered on the 2nd staff line.

The following pitches are played in the same places on your instrument.

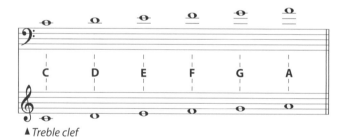

▲ *Treble clef*

Just like the tenor clef, the treble clef is used in the higher ranges of the double bass to avoid too many ledger lines.
The following examples demonstrate how the treble clef eliminates ledger lines.

PRACTICING 3-OCTAVE SCALES

Practice each octave separately

First practice each octave separately. Then connect the octaves to form a continuous three-octave scale. The Roman numerals indicate the position numbers. A dash (–) before a fingering indicates a shift to a new position.

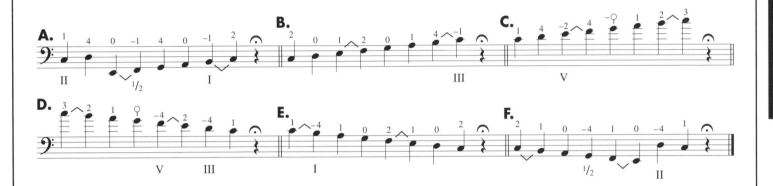

The 24-note system

Adding 3 notes at the beginning and at the end of a three-octave scale can make the scale more versatile for using different bowings. A scale with 24 ascending notes and 24 descending notes can accommodate slurring patterns of 2, 3, 4, 6, 8, 12 and 24 notes.

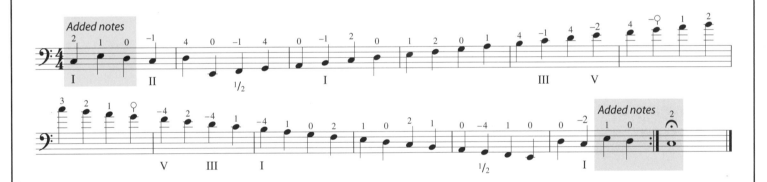

Changing the slur patterns

Different slurring patterns may be easily adapted to the 24-note scale system. Here are some examples using the 24-note C Major scale:

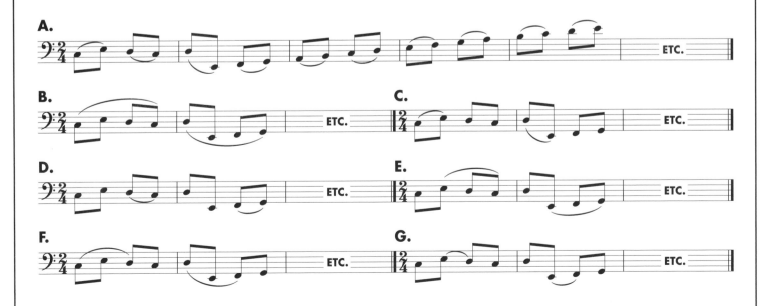

SCALES & ARPEGGIOS

Changing rhythms

Practicing scales with different rhythms helps develop left and right hand facility. Here are some examples using the 24-note C Major scale:

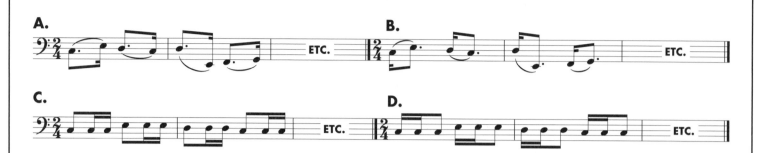

A.   **B.**

C.   **D.**

Changing bowing styles and articulations

Develop better bowing skills by combining scales with different bowing styles and articulations. These examples of *staccato*, *spiccato* and *portato* are shown with the 24-note scale pattern in C Major.

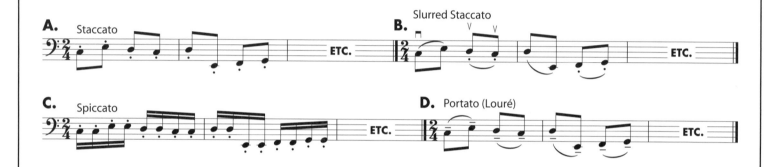

A. Staccato   **B.** Slurred Staccato

C. Spiccato   **D.** Portato (Louré)

Speeding up the scale

Setting a steady tempo with a metronome while decreasing note values is an effective method of learning to play scales faster. In the example below from the 24-note C Major scale, the dark vertical lines indicate metronome clicks. Begin playing at a slow, comfortable tempo, and gradually increase the speed of the metronome as your facility develops.

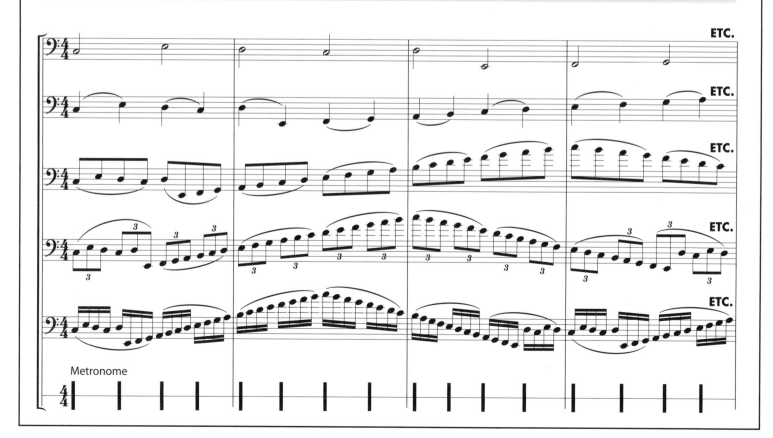

Metronome

DOUBLE BASSES ONLY

SAMPLE ROUTINE FOR PRACTICING 3-OCTAVE SCALES

Here is an example of a complete practice routine for a 3-octave scale in C Major.
Other bowing patterns, articulations and rhythmic variations may also be used.

A. Practice each octave separately

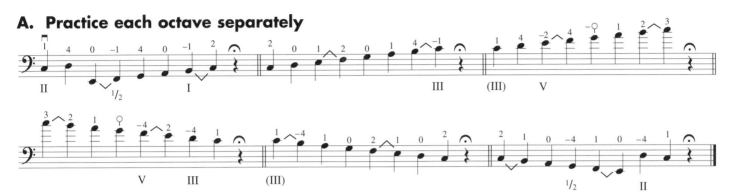

B. Connect the octaves in the 24-note system

C. Change the slur patterns

D. Change rhythms

E. Change bowing styles and articulations

F. Speed up the scale

ySide

SCALES & ARPEGGIOS

THE NECK AND THUMB POSITION

DOUBLE BASSES ONLY

The neck positions (V, V½, VI, VI½, VII) on the double bass are played with the thumb either behind or on the side of the neck. After V½ position the third finger is used in place of the fourth finger. When playing higher than seventh position on the double bass, Roman numerals are rarely used to indicate position.

BASIC THUMB POSITION – D STRING

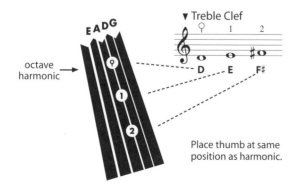

Place thumb at same position as harmonic.

BASIC THUMB POSITION – G STRING

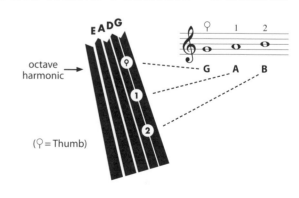

(♀ = Thumb)

3-OCTAVE SCALES AND ARPEGGIOS

MAJOR KEYS

Refer to pages 3–5 ("How To Play 3-Octave Scales/Arpeggios") for a sample practice routine, and for additional bowings, rhythms and articulations that can be applied. Fingerings are printed above the notes, plus the Roman numerals below indicate the position numbers. A dash (–) before a fingering indicates a shift to a new position.

The 24-note system is used for all scales to accommodate slurring patterns of 2, 3, 4, 6, 8, 12 or 24 notes.

1. C MAJOR SCALE

2. C MAJOR ARPEGGIO

3. G MAJOR SCALE

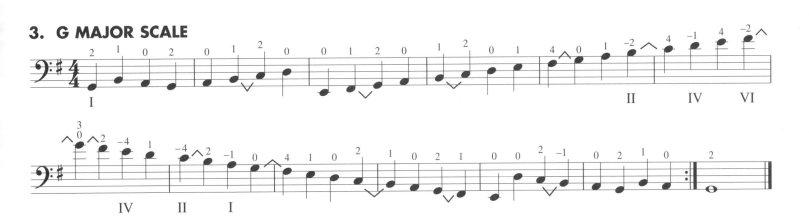

4. G MAJOR ARPEGGIO

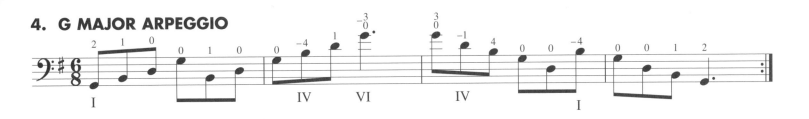

5. D MAJOR SCALE

6. D MAJOR ARPEGGIO

7. A MAJOR SCALE

8. A MAJOR ARPEGGIO

9. E MAJOR SCALE

10. E MAJOR ARPEGGIO

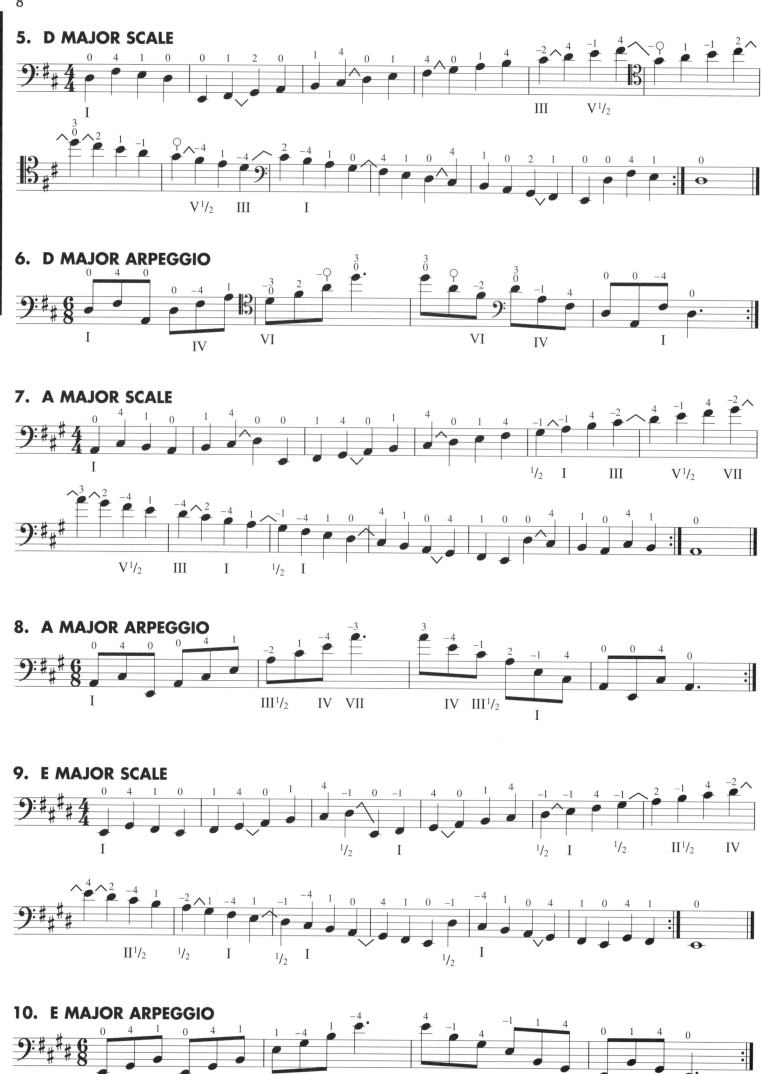

11. B MAJOR SCALE

12. B MAJOR ARPEGGIO

13. F MAJOR SCALE

14. F MAJOR ARPEGGIO

15. B♭ MAJOR SCALE

16. B♭ MAJOR ARPEGGIO

17. E♭ MAJOR SCALE

18. E♭ MAJOR ARPEGGIO

19. A♭ MAJOR SCALE

20. A♭ MAJOR ARPEGGIO

21. D♭ MAJOR SCALE

22. D♭ MAJOR ARPEGGIO

3-OCTAVE SCALES AND ARPEGGIOS

MINOR KEYS

Refer to pages 3–5 ("How To Play 3-Octave Scales/Arpeggios") for a sample practice routine, and for additional bowings, rhythms and articulations that can be applied. Fingerings are printed above the notes, plus the Roman numerals below indicate the position numbers. A dash (–) before a fingering indicates a shift to a new position.

The 24-note system is used for all scales to accommodate slurring patterns of 2, 3, 4, 6, 8, 12 or 24 notes.

23. A MELODIC MINOR SCALE

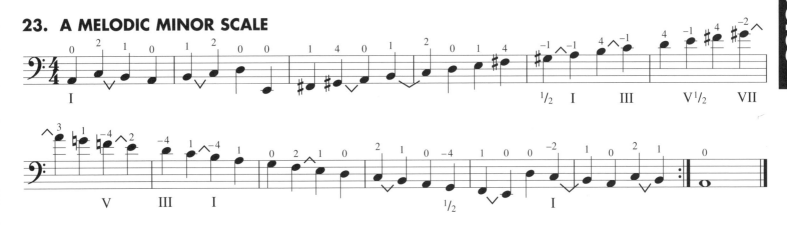

24. A MINOR ARPEGGIO

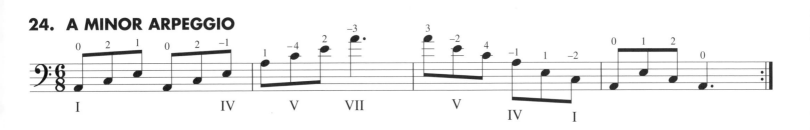

25. E MELODIC MINOR SCALE

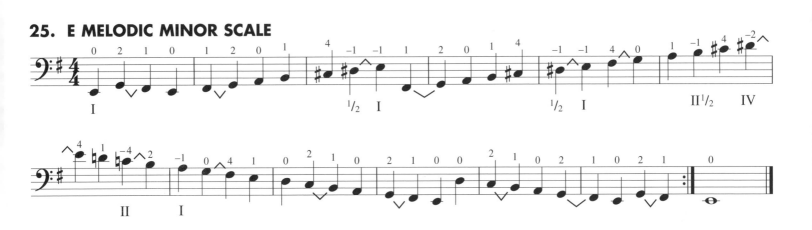

26. E MINOR ARPEGGIO

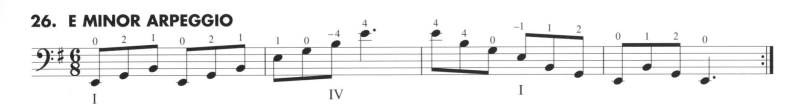

27. B MELODIC MINOR SCALE

28. B MINOR ARPEGGIO

29. F# MELODIC MINOR SCALE

30. F# MINOR ARPEGGIO

31. D MELODIC MINOR SCALE

32. D MINOR ARPEGGIO

33. G MELODIC MINOR SCALE

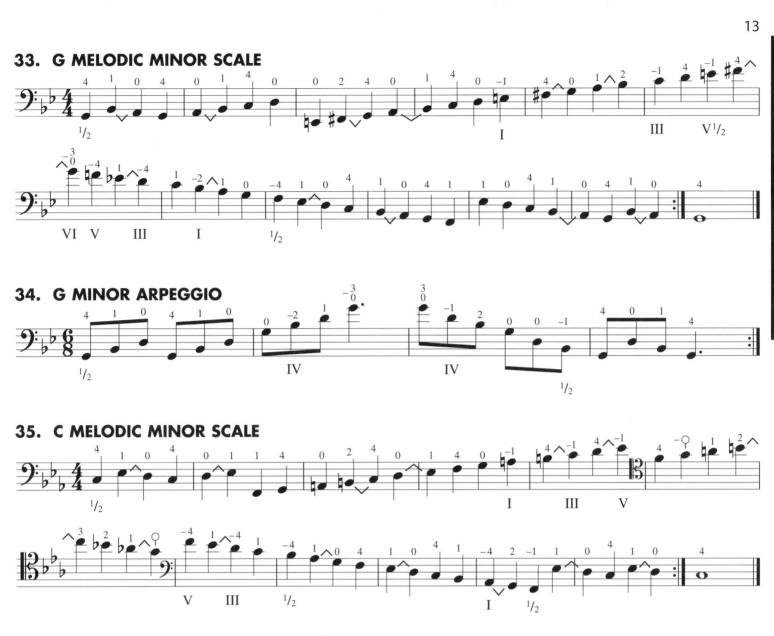

34. G MINOR ARPEGGIO

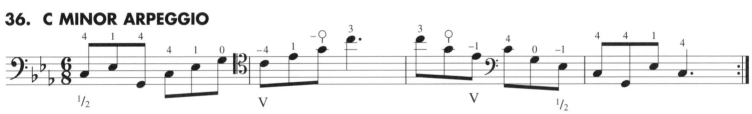

35. C MELODIC MINOR SCALE

36. C MINOR ARPEGGIO

37. F MELODIC MINOR SCALE

38. F MINOR ARPEGGIO

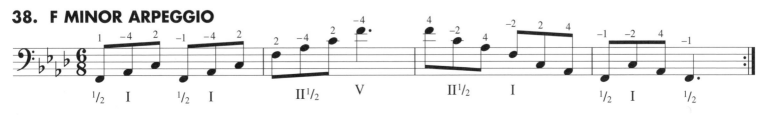

SHIFTING STUDIES

Reminders for shifting...

- Slide your left hand smoothly.
- Move your thumb with your second finger.

SHIFT ON: G and D STRINGS
POSITIONS: I, II, II½, III, IV, V, V½, VI

SHIFT ON: G and D STRINGS
POSITIONS: I, II, II½, III, III½, IV, V½, VI

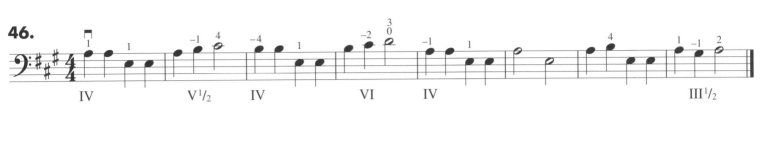

46.

47.

48.

49.

50.

51.

52.

53.

SHIFTING

SHIFT ON: G and D STRINGS
POSITIONS: I, II, III, III½, IV, V

SHIFTING

54.

55.

56.

57.

58.

59.

60.

61.

SHIFT ON: D and A STRINGS
POSITIONS: ½, I, II, III, III½

62.

63.

64.

65.

SHIFT ON: D STRING
POSITIONS: ½, II, II½, III, III½

66.

67.

68.

69.

SHIFTING

REPERTOIRE FOR SHIFTING POSITIONS: ½, I, II, III

Fingerings chosen for technical development.

70. ALLEGRO SPIRITOSO

Jean Baptiste Senaillé

71. CONCERTO GROSSO, OPUS 3, NO. 11

Antonio Vivaldi

SHIFTING

REPERTOIRE FOR SHIFTING
POSITIONS: ½, I, II, II½, III, IV, V, V½

Fingerings chosen for technical development.

72. THE MERRY WIDOW WALTZ

Franz Lehár

73. MOLDAU

Bedrich Smetana

REPERTOIRE FOR SHIFTING
POSITIONS: I, II, III, III½, IV

Fingerings chosen for technical development.

74. TOREADOR SONG (from CARMEN)

Andante

Georges Bizet

75. MELODY IN F

Moderato

Anton Rubinstein

SHIFTING

REPERTOIRE FOR SHIFTING
POSITIONS: ½, I, II, II½, III, IV, V

Fingerings chosen for technical development.

76. SYMPHONY NO. 5 – 4th MOVEMENT

Franz Schubert

77. EINE KLEINE NACHTMUSIK THEME

Wolfgang Amadeus Mozart

SHIFTING

22

SHIFT ON: D STRING
POSITIONS: I, II, II½, III, III½, IV, V, V½

SHIFT ON: A STRING
POSITIONS:

SHIFT ON: G, D, and A STRINGS
POSITIONS: ½, I, II, III½

87.

88.

89.

90.

SHIFT ON: A and E STRINGS
POSITIONS: ½, II, III½

91.

92.

93.

94.

SHIFTING

REPERTOIRE FOR SHIFTING
POSITIONS: ½, I, II, III, IV, V

Fingerings chosen for technical development.

95. SONATA NO. 12

Niccolo Paganini

96. ETUDE

DeBeriot

97. OVERTURE TO ROSAMUNDE

Franz Schubert

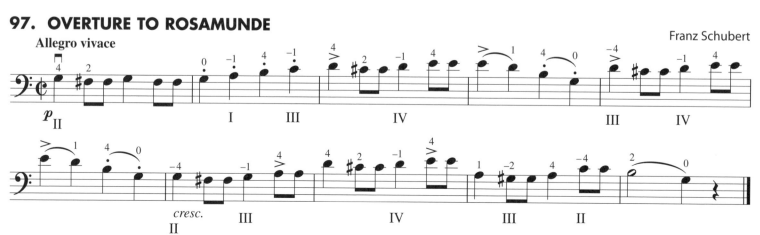

SHIFT ON: A STRING
POSITIONS: ½, I, II, III, III½, IV

98.

99.

100.

101.

SHIFT ON: G and D STRINGS
POSITIONS: I, II, II½, III, IV, V, V½

102.

103.

104.

105.

SHIFTING

SHIFT ON: D and A STRINGS
POSITIONS: ½, I, II, II½, III, III½, IV

SHIFT ON: G, D, and A STRINGS
POSITIONS: ½, I, II, II½, III, III½

REPERTOIRE FOR SHIFTING POSITIONS: ½, I, II, III, V

Fingerings chosen for technical development.

126. AMARYLLIS

Andante

Henri Ghys

127. SLAVONIC DANCE NO 1

Presto

Antonin Dvorak

128. SYMPHONY NO. 1 – 2nd MOVEMENT

Andante cantabile con moto

Ludwig van Beethoven

129. THE AMERICAN PATROL

Allegretto

F. W. Meacham

SHIFTING

REPERTOIRE FOR SHIFTING
POSITIONS: ½, II, III, III½, IV, V

Fingerings chosen for technical development.

130. ALLELUIA (from EXULTATE JUBILANTE)

Wolfgang Amadeus Mozart

131. LITTLE FUGUE IN G MINOR

Johann Sebastian Bach

132. AIR (from WATER MUSIC)

George Frideric Handel

SHIFTING

REPERTOIRE FOR SHIFTING POSITIONS: ½, I, II, II½, III, IV

Fingerings chosen for technical development.

133. LA FOLIA

A. Corelli

134. PAVANE FOR A DEAD PRINCESS

Maurice Ravel

135. SYMPHONY NO. 29 THEME

Wolfgang Amadeus Mozart

SHIFT ON: G and D STRINGS
POSITIONS: ½, I, II½, III, III½, IV

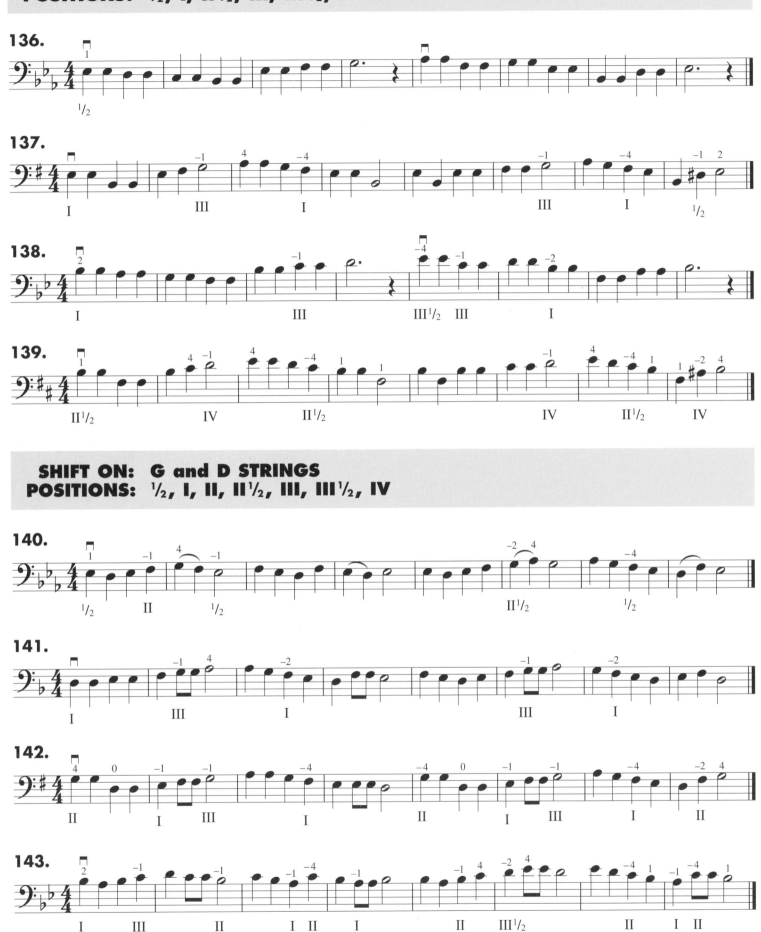

SHIFT ON: G and D STRINGS
POSITIONS: ½, I, II, II½, III, III½, IV

REPERTOIRE FOR SHIFTING POSITIONS: ½, I, II, III, IV

Fingerings chosen for technical development.

145. SYMPHONY NO. 5 – 4th MOVEMENT

Ludwig van Beethoven

146. THE BARBER OF SEVILLE OVERTURE

Gioachino Rossini

SHIFT ON: D and A STRINGS
POSITIONS: ½, I, II

147.

148.

149.

150.

151.

152.

REPERTOIRE FOR SHIFTING
POSITIONS: I, II, II½, III, III½

Fingerings chosen for technical development.

153. IN THE HALL OF THE MOUNTAIN KING

A'lla marcia e molto marcato

Edvard Grieg

SHIFTING

SHIFT ON: G and D STRINGS
POSITIONS: ½, I, II, III, IV, V, VI

154.

IV   VI V   VI   IV   V IV   V   VI   IV

155.

I   III   I   III   I   II

156.

I   III   II   I   III   II   I

157.

I   II   I   II   ½   II   ½   II   ½

SHIFT ON: D and A STRINGS
POSITIONS: ½, I, II, III

158.

I   III   I   III   I

159.

I   III   I   III   I   II

160.

I   III   II I   III   II   I

161.

I   II   I   II   I   ½

REPERTOIRE FOR SHIFTING POSITIONS: ½, I

Fingerings chosen for technical development.

162. THE MASTERSINGER OF NUREMBERG

Richard Wagner

163. FARANDOLE

Georges Bizet

SHIFTING

RHYTHM AND BOWING STUDIES

SIXTEENTH NOTE STUDIES

NOTE DURATION CHART

6/8 RHYTHM STUDIES

NOTE DURATION CHART

1 + 2 + 3 + **4** + 5 + 6 +   1 + 2 + 3 + **4** + 5 + 6 +

DOTTED RHYTHM STUDIES

NOTE DURATION CHART

SYNCOPATION STUDIES

NOTE DURATION CHART

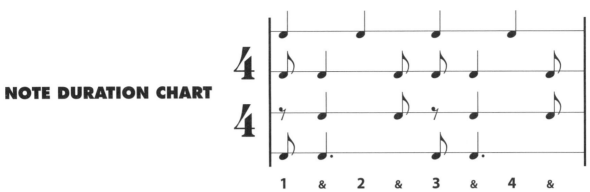

185.

186.

187.

188.

189.

190.

191.

THE BAROQUE ERA (CA. 1600 – 1750)

Following the Renaissance, music and the arts (and even clothing) became more elaborate and dramatic during the *Baroque* era (about 1600–1750). Like the fancy decorations of Baroque church architecture, melodies were often played with ornamentation such as *trills* and *grace notes*. Rhythms became faster and more complex with time signatures and bar lines. Our now familiar major and minor scales formed the basis for harmony, and chords were standardized to what we often hear today.

The harpsichord became the most popular keyboard instrument, with players often *improvising* (making up) their parts using the composer's chords and bass line. Violin making reached new heights in Italy. Operas, ballets and small orchestras were beginning to take shape, as composers specified the instruments, tempos and dynamics to be performed. Johann Sebastian Bach, George Frideric Handel and Antonio Vivaldi were among the important composers of the *Baroque* era.

Johann Sebastian Bach

BAROQUE STYLE

Although music notation was becoming standardized during the Baroque era, there were many details left to be interpreted by the performers. For instance, 4/4 (or Common Time) and 2/2 (or Cut Time) were sometimes written interchangeably. In medium to fast tempos, the *performers* must determine whether the quarter note or the half note is the actual pulse. Normally, the **"running" notes** (4 to a beat) are played with *detaché* strokes, while **"walking" notes** (2 to a beat) should be separated using a *martelé* bowing stroke.

- **Quarter note** pulse indicated by "running" 16ths:
- Bowing style with a **quarter note** pulse:

 =

- **Half note** pulse indicated by "running" 8ths:
- Bowing style with a **half note** pulse:

 =

- **Ornamentation** was often written into the music, but could also be improvised by the performers. The most common musical ornament is the *trill*, which usually begins one scale step above the written note.

- **Dynamic changes** were sometimes left to the creativity of the performers, since there was no standardized notation for crescendo and decrescendo. In today's orchestras, players rely on the judgment of their conductor so that everyone plays with a unified interpretation.

Using the guidelines above, play the following exercises in a Baroque style.

STYLE

196. MESSIAH OVERTURE (excerpt)

George Frideric Handel

DOUBLE BASSES ONLY

Additional material from "Messiah Overture" for study and practice

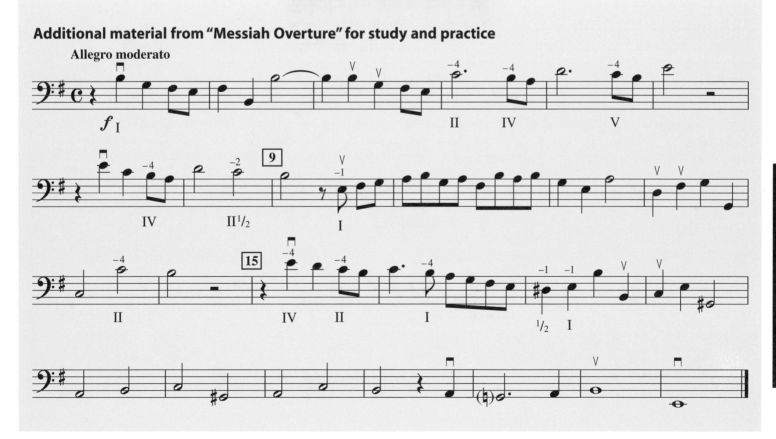

STYLE

197. CONCERTO FOR TWO VIOLINS AND ORCHESTRA (excerpt)

Johann Sebastian Bach

DOUBLE BASSES ONLY

Additional material from "Concerto for Two Violins and Orchestra" for study and practice

THE CLASSICAL ERA (CA. 1750 – 1825)

Wolfgang Amadeus Mozart

The *Classical* era, from about 1750 to the early 1800's, was a time of great contrasts. While patriots fought for the rights of the common people in the American and French revolutions, composers were employed to entertain wealthy nobles and aristocrats. In contrast to the *Baroque* era, music became simpler and more elegant, with melodies often flowing over accompaniment patterns in regular 4-bar phrases. Like the architecture of ancient *Classical* Greece, music was fit together in "building blocks" by balancing one phrase against another, or one entire section against another.

The piano replaced the harpsichord, and became the most popular instrument for the *concerto* (solo) with orchestra accompaniment. The string quartet became the favorite form of *chamber* (small group) music, and orchestra concerts featured *symphonies* (longer compositions with 4 contrasting parts or *movements*). Wolfgang Amadeus Mozart and Franz Josef Haydn were leading composers in the *Classical* era. Toward the end of this era, Ludwig van Beethoven's changing musical style led the way toward the more emotional and personal expression of *Romantic* music.

CLASSICAL STYLE

In medium to fast tempos, lightness and articulation with the bow are the most important aspects of Classical style. The melody should always predominate, producing a clean, clear tone.

- **Eighth Notes,** with or without staccato dots, are usually played spiccato.

- **Quarter Notes** are normally separated, stopping the bow slightly between the notes.

- **Syncopation** is always played with separation, and with emphasis on the longer notes.

- In **2-Note Slurs,** the "second" notes of each pair are played lighter and shorter.

- A **grace note** is often played *on the beat* and slurred into the note it displaces.

- **Slur-Lift-Spiccato:** The last note in this slur is the transition from on the string to spiccato. Lift the bow at the end of the slur.

Original editions of Classical literature were often printed with very few articulation marks. Using the guidelines above, play the following exercises in a Classical style.

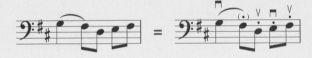

201. DIVERTIMENTO, K. 136 – 3rd MOVEMENT (excerpt)

Wolfgang Amadeus Mozart
Composed 1772, Salzburg, Austria

DOUBLE BASSES ONLY

Additional material from "Divertimento" for study and practice

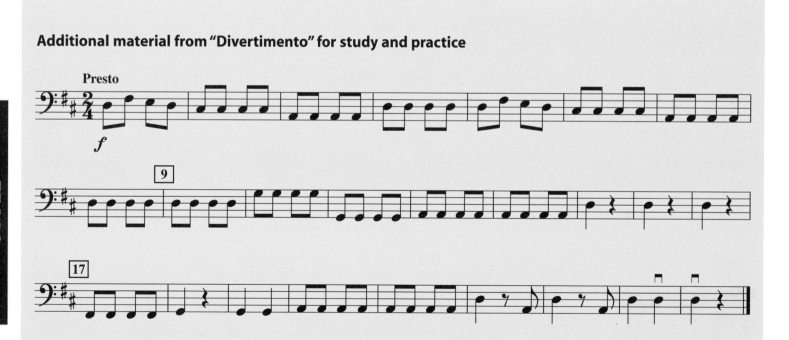

202. QUARTET NO. 3 IN G MAJOR, K. 156 (excerpt)

Wolfgang Amadeus Mozart

DOUBLE BASSES ONLY

Additional material from "Quartet No. 3 in G Major" for study and practice

THE ROMANTIC ERA (CA. 1820 – 1900)

The last compositions of Beethoven were among the first in the new *Romantic* era, lasting from the early 1800's to about 1900. No longer employed by churches or nobles, composers became free from Classical restraints, and expressed their personal emotions through their music. Instead of simple titles like *Concerto* or *Symphony,* they would often add descriptive titles like *Witches' Dance* or *To The New World.* Orchestras became larger, including nearly all the standard instruments we now use. Composers began to write much more difficult and complex music, featuring more "colorful" instrument combinations and harmonies.

Nationalism was an important trend in this era. Composers used folk music and folk legends (especially in Russia, eastern Europe and Scandinavia) to identify their music with their native lands. Today's concert audiences still generally prefer the drama of Romantic music to any other type. Ludwig van Beethoven, Johannes Brahms, Peter I. Tchaikowsky, Antonin Dvorak, and Edvard Grieg were among the many important composers of this era.

Peter I. Tchaikowsky

ROMANTIC STYLE

Romantic music requires a variety of left and right hand techniques to capture its drama and expressiveness. Extreme dynamic levels which may include very slow and very fast dynamic changes, heavy accents, and long sustained phrases require an array of special bow control skills. In addition to coping with the more chromatic nature of the music, the left hand must also vary the speed and intensity of vibrato.

■ Vary the **dynamics** and **tone color** by changing bow speed, pressure and placement, *plus* vibrato speed and intensity:

■ Heavy accents are sometimes played with a **"hammered"** stroke:

■ **Long sustained phrases** generally require a slower bow speed. Adjust your bow pressure and **contact point** (placement) on the string to help express the required dynamics and tone color:

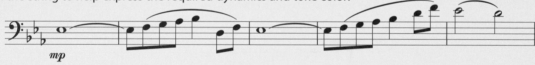

■ A special bowing such as **portato** (louré), **ricochet, sul ponticello** or **sul tasto** may be required to express a musical phrase. If not marked by the composer, the conductor and concertmaster will make these selections for the orchestra.

Using the guidelines above, play the following exercises in a Romantic style.

206. SERENADE FOR STRINGS – 1st MOVEMENT

Peter I. Tchaikowsky

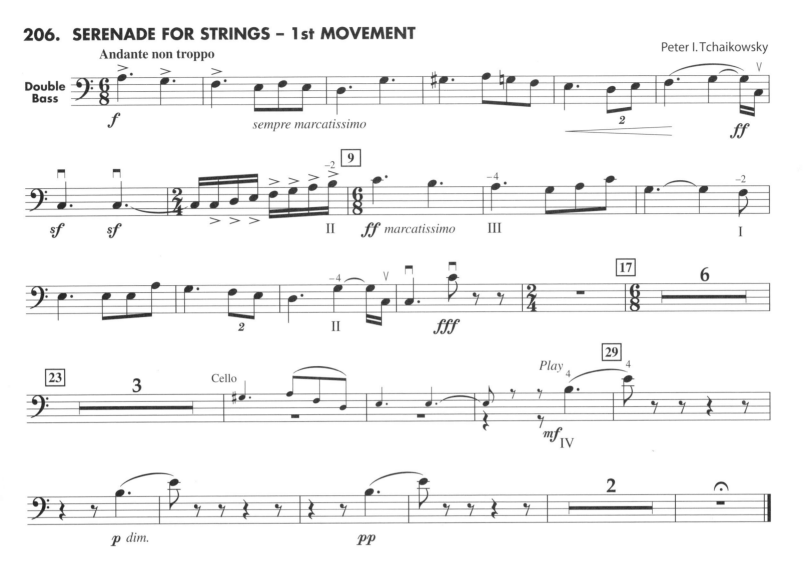

DOUBLE BASSES ONLY

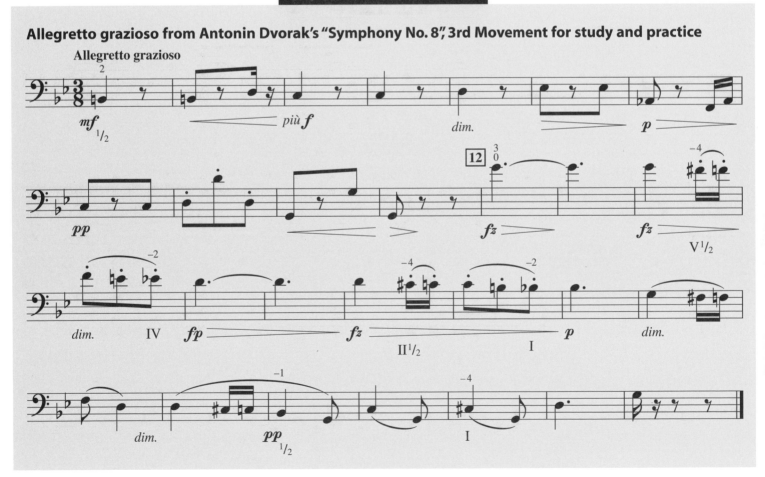

Allegretto grazioso from Antonin Dvorak's "Symphony No. 8", 3rd Movement for study and practice

STYLE

207. ÅSE'S DEATH (from PEER GYNT SUITE NO. 1 – excerpt)

Edvard Grieg

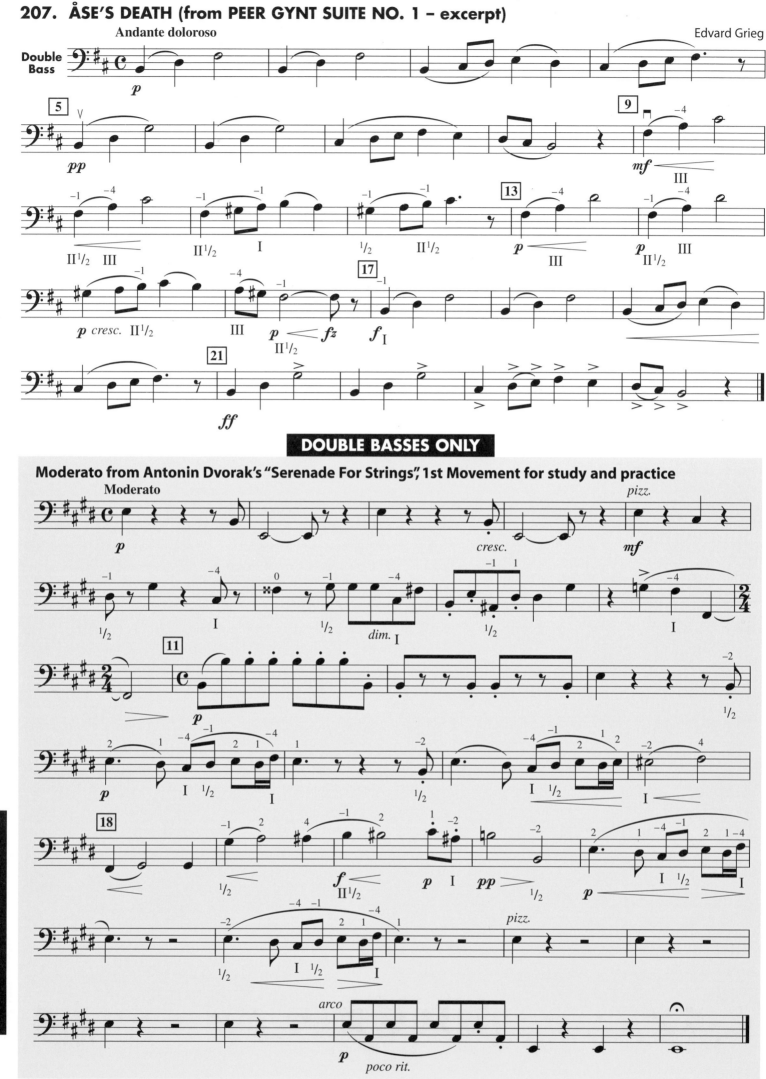

DOUBLE BASSES ONLY

Moderato from Antonin Dvorak's "Serenade For Strings", 1st Movement for study and practice